The Fullness of Time
by Kim Skinner

ISBN 978-0-9913399-4-5

Published by
Two Stepping, Inc.
8280 Princeton Square Blvd. W., Suite 9
Jacksonville, FL. 32256 USA

http://twostepping.com

Please visit Kim Skinner online at
http://www.kimskinner.com

the fullness of TIME

A TIMELY REFLECTION WHILE THE CLOCK IS TICKING

Kim Skinner

Foreword

written by Dawn Emerick, Ed.D

Time. At first glance, it's a short and uncomplicated word. Only four letters. When written, the word is easy on a reader's eyes and on a writer's grip. When transferred from ink to paper, the word takes up very little space. However, books like *The Fullness of Time* remind us all that time is not for the faint of heart. Time is indeed a very complicated four letter word. When you think about it, time is the only word that represents the past, the present, and the future with each approaching and passing second. Time is intrusive, precious, hurtful, expensive, sacred, absent, poetic, short, and symbolic. Kim Skinner establishes a literary time capsule with *The Fullness of Time*. Her descriptive narrative and complimentary pictures take us on a journey through the many dimensions, definitions, and interpretations of time. *The Fullness of Time* inspires us all to recall, reflect, smile, cry and embrace all that's good about time.

When Kim asked me to write the foreword to her book, I was so honored. *The Fullness of Time* struck a chord with me the minute I read the quote from former First Lady Barbara Bush:

"At the end of your life, you will never regret not having passed more tests, not winning one more verdict or not closing one more deal. You will regret time not spent with the husband, a friend, a child, or a parent."

The Fullness of Time is the perfect read for countless others who seek ways to understand and to manage time. For many years, time was my most reliable friend. It was supportive. Endearing. Nurturing. Later on in life, however, time became a bit unforgiving. I took time for granted while investing in my family and career. I worked hard to reach the level of success all Type A personalities desire. For the last decade, I have woken up every morning after a solid four hours of sleep, eager to be the high-powered CEO, the transformational boss, the cool parent, the attentive wife, the loyal friend, the committed volunteer, and the inspiring mentor during the other 20 hours. Meanwhile, my house was a mess. I had weeks' worth of laundry to do, and my car was an active science experiment. Still, though, my nails were always impeccable. My roots were always colored. I dressed to the nines, and I attended all the best socials across the country. Many asked me, "How do you balance it all, Dawn?" I typically responded by sincerely acknowledging the great support system I had at home. But the truth was, I hadn't balanced this train wreck in years, and I had found myself building a Hold-On Legacy: A legacy of putting the most important people in your life and their time on hold while you attend to a detail in your work life. I'm sure you know exactly what I am referring

to. We are all building Hold-On Legacies. Here are some examples of mine:

- "HOLD-ON, Melanie. Let me send this email real quick."
- "HOLD-ON, Tasha, let Mommy finish this call."
- "HOLD-ON, Al, I really need to finish this proposal."
- "HOLD-ON, Pam. Oh shoot... I need to call you back."
- "HOLD-ON, Jimmy, I've gotta take this call."
- "HOLD-ON, Tre, I have to close this deal. I'll meet you at Starbucks instead."

On March 22, 2014, time changed me forever. This was the day I called the Chair of my Board of Directors and told her I was resigning. After years of rebuilding the company, I felt I had done enough. The Board of Directors, staff, and business community were shocked that I chose to step down right when the company had reached its apex and my career was in full throttle.

Certainly there had to be more to the story. Speculation was widespread. Someone actually created a hashtag #WhatsDawnDoing. But, there was no controversy. I was physically, mentally and spiritually exhausted.

Time won.

Kim's commitment to her faith, to her family and to others sparkles on each page. She has taken an imperfect word and created a photo album, a history and literature lesson, and cultural and spiritual journey rolled into one. She reminds you of songs and poetic passages that bring you back to where you were and who you were with. More importantly, *The Fullness of Time* speaks to each of us in a way that is uniquely us. I guess in the end, that makes us all winners.

Congratulations, Kim.

Dawn Emerick, Ed.D

Wife, Mother, National Speaker, University Professor, Principle, Impact Partners LLC

The writer operates at a peculiar crossroads where time and place and eternity somehow meet. His problem is to find that location.

Flannery O'Connor

Time

(tahym)

Noun

1. The system of those sequential relations that any event has to any other, as past, present, or future, in definite and continuous duration regarded as that in which events succeed one another.

2. The duration in which all things happen, or a precise instant that something happens.

3. The present life; existence in this world as contrasted with immortal life; definite, as contrasted with infinite.

Time is the most valuable thing a man can spend.
- Theophrastus

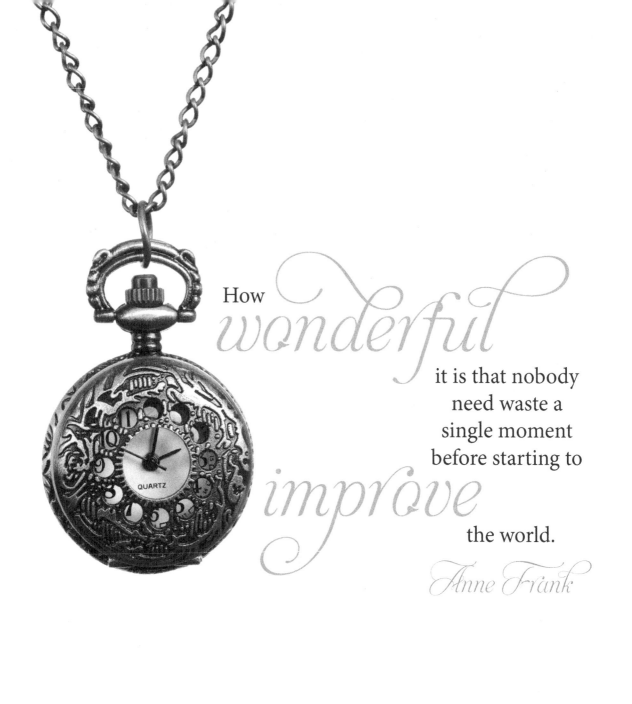

How *wonderful* it is that nobody
need waste a
single moment
before starting to
improve
the world.

Anne Frank

Fullness:
distention, roundness, swelling, voluptuousness

I understand fullness. Fullness of grocery carts, laundry baskets, incoming mail… My cup runneth over.

Subjectively, my heart knows fullness. Friendships and family and undeserved kindness… Fullness of joy seems to spring forth unbidden but most welcome.

So what am I to make of "the fullness of time "? If anything, time seems flimsy to me. It can be stretched and crammed and cursed and ignored. Appreciation of it seems to disappear as quickly as it begins.

But I remember such a time!

When the time was ripe I delivered each of my five children. An intricately balanced number of details fit together to produce each wonder boasting ten fingers and ten toes. So it does not seem surprising that this phrase is used in a Christmas Bible passage announcing the birth of the Christ child.

The fullness of time reminds me of past times celebrating the Christmas season as one of the traditions of my people. Past memories flood to the present and resonate even now because this birth promised, long ago, to bring the infinite One into our finite lives today. Past meets present and points beyond!

Moreover, the time is always right for me to keep time with "Love" itself. I need it; to acknowledge it, yearn for it, receive it, account it, give it.

"The Fullness of Time" is my gift to you.

But when the fullness of time had come, God sent his son, born of woman, born under the law, to redeem those who were under the law, so that we might receive adoption as sons."

(Galatians 4: 4-5 ESV)

Time is too slow for those who wait,
Too swift for those who fear,
Too long for those who grieve,
Too short for those who rejoice,
But for those who love, time is ETERNITY.

Henry Van Dyke

Three things you
cannot recover in life
The word after it is said
The moment after it is missed
And time after it is gone

Africaans	maal, keer, tyd, uur
Danish	tid, time, gang
Dutch	keer, maal
Finnish	aika, kerta, tunti
German	zeitlich, zeit
Italian	tempo, epoca, cronologico, marchio, lezione, tattoo
Latin	aetas, tempus temponis, hora, tractus
Norwegian	tid, time
Portuguese	tempo

TIME TRANSLATIONS

The future is something which everyone reaches at
the rate of 60 minutes an hour,
whatever he does,
whoever he is.

C.S.Lewis

WHAT WE DO IN LIFE ECHOES IN ETERNITY.

SPOKEN BY MAXIMUS IN THE MOVIE, GLADIATOR

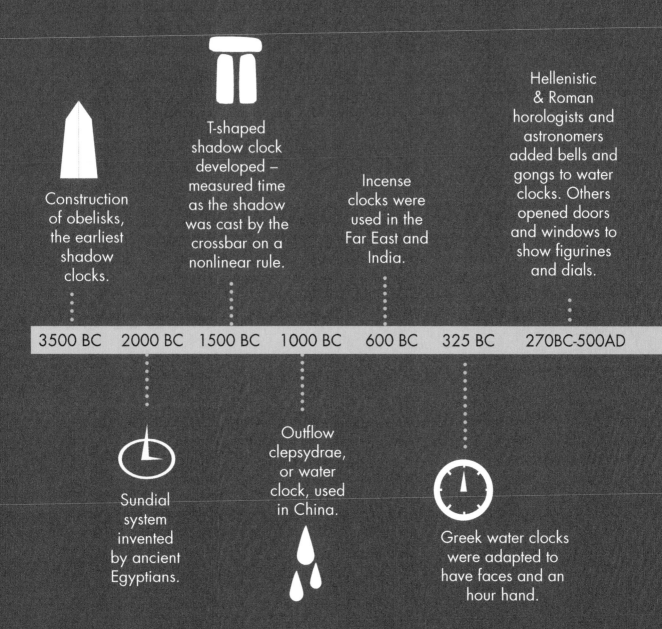

Construction of obelisks, the earliest shadow clocks.

T-shaped shadow clock developed – measured time as the shadow was cast by the crossbar on a nonlinear rule.

Incense clocks were used in the Far East and India.

Hellenistic & Roman horologists and astronomers added bells and gongs to water clocks. Others opened doors and windows to show figurines and dials.

3500 BC   2000 BC   1500 BC   1000 BC   600 BC   325 BC   270BC-500AD

Sundial system invented by ancient Egyptians.

Outflow clepsydrae, or water clock, used in China.

Greek water clocks were adapted to have faces and an hour hand.

Chinese astronomer, Su Song, built the first clock tower in Kaifeng City.

Salisbury Cathedral Clock was created, claims to be the oldest working clock in the world.

Clock dials were made to show minutes and seconds.

Medieval Christian monks became skillful mechanical clock makers.

| 500 AD | 850 AD | 900 AD | 1100 AD | 1386 AD | 1400s AD | 1475 AD |

Incense clocks were made in Japan. One still exists in Shosoin.

The first geared clock was invented in Islamic Iberia.

Middle Ages produced many striking clocks used primarily for religious events.

1707, four naval ships
ran aground - British
government offered
a huge reward for
accurate chronometer.

Galileo
Galilee studied
the pendulum
to be used for
regulating a
clock.

Pocket
watches
invented.

John Harrison built
the first Marine
chronometer and
perfected it over the
next 30 years. Tested
by his son in 1761 -
after 10 weeks, it was
accurate to 5 seconds.

| 1522 | 1580 | 1656 | 1675 | 1700s | 1707 | 1735 | 1751 | 1800 |

Portuguese
navigator
Ferdinand
Magellan used
18 hour glasses
on each ship
during his
circumnavigation
of the globe in
1522.

Dutch scientist
Christian
Huygens finally
created a
very accurate
pendulum
system.

+/=

Equation clocks
were made.

Queen
Elizabeth I
of England
received a
wristwatch
(described as an
arm watch) from
Robert Dudley.

Switzerland
established
itself as a
clockmaking
center as
an influx of
Huguenot
craftsmen
came
committed to
high quality
machine-
made
watches.

Scottish clockmaker Alexander Payne invented the electric clock on January 11, 1841, and patented it.

The U.S. National Bureau of Standards built a prototype ammonia maser device (atomic clock). International System of Units standardized the properties of cesium – accurate to 30 billionths of a second per year.

1814   1840   1927   1949   1967   1969

Sir Francis Ronalds of London invented the forerunner to an electric clock.

The first quartz crystal clock was built.

The first accurate atomic clock built in the UK.

Seiko produced the world's first quartz wristwatch, the Astron.

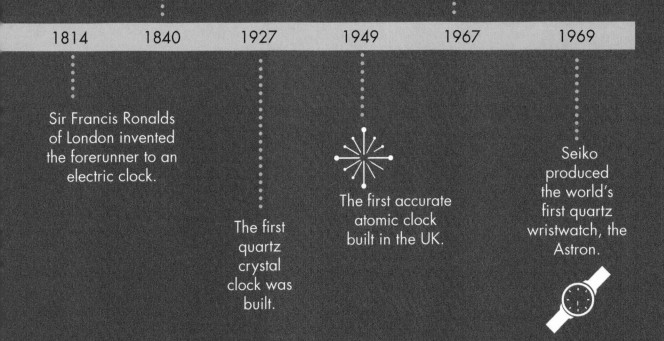

Time heals griefs and quarrels, for we change and are no longer the same persons. Neither the offender nor the offended art anymore themselves.

Blaise Pascal

The present is the ever moving shadow that divides yesterday from tomorrow. In that lies hope.

Frank Lloyd Wright

Time is at once the most valuable and the most perishable of all our possessions.

John Randolph

All we have to decide is what to do with the time
that is given to us.

J.R.R Tolkien

Only the one who isn't rowing has time to rock the boat.

Jean-Paul Sartre

The hardest years of life are those between
ten and seventy.

Helen Hunt

The trouble with talking too fast is you may say
something you haven't thought of yet.

Ann Landers

DOES ANYBODY REALLY KNOW WHAT TIME IT IS?

AS I WAS WALKING DOWN THE STREET ONE DAY
A MAN CAME UP TO ME AND ASKED ME WHAT THE TIME WAS
THAT WAS ON MY WATCH
AND I SAID

DOES ANYBODY REALLY KNOW WHAT TIME IT IS?
DOES ANYBODY REALLY CARE?
IF SO I CAN'T IMAGINE WHY
WE'VE ALL GOT TIME ENOUGH TO CRY
OH NO, NO

AND I WAS WALKING DOWN THE STREET ONE DAY
A PRETTY LADY LOOKED AT ME AND SAID HER DIAMOND WATCH
HAD STOPPED COLD DEAD.
AND I SAID

DOES ANYBODY REALLY KNOW WHAT TIME IT IS?
DOES ANYBODY REALLY CARE?
IF SO I CAN'T IMAGINE WHY
WE'VE ALL GOT TIME ENOUGH TO CRY
OH NO, NO

AND I WAS WALKING DOWN THE STREET ONE DAY
BEING PUSHED AND SHOVED BY PEOPLE TRYING TO BEAT THE CLOCK
OH, SO I JUST DON'T KNOW

The future is made up of the same stuff as the present.
Simone Weil

I have made this letter longer than usual, only because
I have not had the time to make it shorter.
Blaise Pascal

We are all, at times, unconscious prophets.
Charles Spurgeon

TIME

THE WEEKLY NEWSMAGAZINE

MAN OF THE YEAR
All that He has made you he made, but cursed that cruel
(Foreign News)

Ninety years ago,

two Yale graduates collaborated to launch the very first
Time Magazine on March 3, 1923. Today, *Time* has the world's
largest circulation for any weekly newsmagazine, reaching
25 million readers, both at home and abroad.

Time's "Person of the Year" recipients are selected who,
for good or ill, have most affected our world over the past year.

My favorite things in life don't cost any money.
It's really clear that the most precious
resource we all have is time.

Steve Jobs

At the end of your life, you will never regret not having passed more tests, not winning one more verdict or not closing one more deal. You will regret time not spent with the husband, a friend, a child, or a parent.

- *Barbara Bush*

Crossing The Bar

by Alfred Lord Tennyson

Sunset and evening star,
And one clear call for me!
And may there be no meaning of the bar,
When I put out to sea.

But such a tide as moving seems asleep,
Too full for sound and foam,
When that which drew from out the boundless deep
Turns again home.

Twilight and evening bell,
And after that this dark!
And may there be no sadness of farewell,
When I embark;

For though from out our bourne of Time and Peace
The flood may bear me far,
I hope to see my Pilot face-to-face
When I have crossed the bar.

The first literary reference to a clock is found in the poem, "Paradiso" by Dante Alighieri

No one ever wants to hear the words, "I'm sorry but you have cancer." For my friend Joyce, it was as if time stood still.

Joyce and her husband were at the top of their careers and seemed to have their whole lives in front of them. Their only child had just celebrated his second birthday, but the diagnosis of a rare form of bone cancer changed everything.

Seven years later, at a new parent school luncheon, an electric wheelchair buzzed right up to me. It was inhabited by a beautiful blonde woman with soulful blue eyes that sparkled brightly.

"I seem to be one of the new parents here

When Time Ran Out

today," she said as she extended her hand to me. "My name is Joyce."

At the time I was blissfully unaware that the clock had started ticking. Our six-year friendship seemed to fly by yet, at times, it progressed with agonizing slowness. Her determined strength through surgery after surgery amazed me. She amazed everyone she met. Her laugh was rich and infectious. Her heavy tears mingled with those, like me, who loved her.

Time pressed in and would not be ignored. It asserted itself awkwardly, where it had once been casually tolerated. It abrasively probed for answers.

How can a mother willingly let go of her husband and son?

What does one do when faith and stubborn strength are not enough to stop the onslaught of cancer?

Is the time ever right to stop fighting?

Her last weeks were spent at home. One afternoon she invited me to climb into bed with her. She always handled awkward moments like the CPA that she was. She called 'em like she saw 'em and walked me through it one step at a time.

Me (in bed with you) on my husband's side (equals) awkward and funny!

Holding hands we remembered times of hilarity and adventure. We laughed as tears dripped into our ears.

But she was preparing to leave.

"You're my best friend," she said. "I will see you again."

And I believed her. So many of us did. How could we not? Her love and strength and person could not possibly dissolve upon her last breath. We began, strangely, to connect with her somewhere beyond time.

She may be outside the time I presently inhabit, but I will set my watch by the hope she professed. Time cannot silence the heartiness of her laugh or diminish the loving passion in her heart. Time can be both a gift and an enemy, but time can be conquered. I learned that from Joyce.

I saw Eternity the other night,
Like a great ring of pure and endless light,
All calm, as it was bright,
And round beneath it, Time, in hours, days, years,
Driven by the spheres,
Like a vast shadow moved, in which the world
And all her train were hurled.

Madeleine L'Engle

How can the past and future be, when the past no longer
is, and the future is not yet? As for the present, if it were
always present and never moved on to become the past,
it would not be time, but eternity.

Augustine of Hippo

Cinema Time

High noon / 1952
From here to Eternity / 1953
Same time next year / 1978
Nine To Five / 1980
Somewhere in time / 1981
Back to the future / 1985
The land before time / 1988
The second time around / 1991
A time to kill / 1996

Killing Time or Keeping Time?

I'm late! I'm late! For a very important date!
No time to say hello, goodbye! I'm late!
I'm late! I'm late! I'm late!
And when I wave, I lose the time I save
My fuzzy ears and whiskers
Took me too much time to shave.

I run and then I hop, hop, hop.
I wish that I could fly.
There's danger if I dare to stop
And here's the reason why you see,
I'm overdue. I'm in a rabbit stew.
Can't even say "Goodbye", "Hello"
I'm late! I'm late! I'm late!

I'M LATE FROM ALICE IN WONDERLAND (1951)

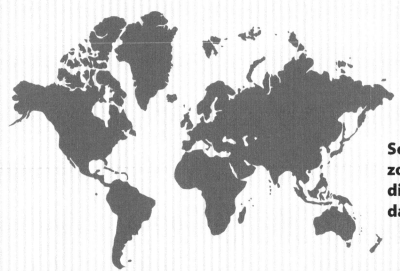

Scientists created 24 time zones to accommodate the differences of night and day throughout the earth.

TIME ZONES

- China and the USA are roughly the same size but China claims only one time zone even though it spans the longitudes of five standard zones.

- The UTC or Co-ordinated Universal Time is based on the caesium atomic clock, invented in 1954. Most scientists prefer this point in time. In practice, the differences between UTC and Zulu time are measured in seconds.

Daylight Savings Time (DST) was standardized in the United States by the Uniform Time Act in 1966.

- Pilots flying internationally synchronize their watches using Zulu time. Located at Greenwich Observatory, London, Zulu (Z), sets the standard for International communication. This 0° line of longitude became the official singular world Meridian in 1884.

Benjamin Franklin was the first to conceive the idea of daylight savings time.

The U.S. has six time zones: Eastern, Central, Mountain, Pacific, Hawaii, and Alaska.

Only one state in the continental USA does not observe daylight savings time: Arizona

- Those industrious Germans inhabited the first country to officially adopt a system of daylight savings time. Germany (April 1916) was followed by Great Britain (May 1916) and many subsequently fell in line. Today 70 countries observe some sort of daylight savings time.

- "Waste of Daylight" was a published pamphlet written in 1907 by a London builder, William Willett. He died before his dream would become a reality.

- Throughout the world, farmers consistently complain about DST. That extra hour of darkness in the morning is inconvenient and disruptive to the folks required to work alongside the sun's patterns.

When does the clock" fall back" or "spring forward"?
The official changeover time is 2:00 AM.

The Most Expensive Watch in the World

$30,000,000.00

(Yes, that's thirty million dollars for one single watch!)

A lover of the French Queen, Marie Antoinette, commissioned Abraham-Louis Breguet in 1782, to create this masterpiece. It was completed 45 years later by Breguet's son. Unfortunately, this was four years after time had run out for his father. The gift was also 34 years too late for the queen, who faced the guillotine in 1793.

This masterpiece was stolen in the late 1900s and miraculously reappeared in 2007.

Encased in gold, the intricate mechanical workings run efficiently and mesmerize its admirers. Breguet used Sapphire to lower the friction within its parts. (Another handy use for sapphires... who knew?)

You won't find this offered on eBay, but it may be viewed at the L. A. Meyer Museum any time at your convenience.

Seize the day!

The first Black Forest cuckoo clock was created in 1630, in the village of Triberg, Germany. Mr. Franz Kettler was credited as the original creator.

In nature the actual cuckoo bird announces that time is right for spring.

Beethoven included the cuckoo in his song in Pastoral Symphony.

In each language the bird's name corresponds to the sound of its call.
France: Coucou
Holland: Koekoek
Germany: Kuckuck
Japan: Kak-ko

Sadly, these birds are squatters. After another bird has labored to build her nest and has begun laying eggs, that sneaky cuckoo bird takes advantage of the other mother's time away and lays her own eggs. Her job is done and she irresponsibly flies away, allowing her chicks to be incubated by another, more responsible and less cuckoo, mother.

cuckoo clocks

In "The Sound of Music" the von Trapp children sang their farewell song about the cuckoo.

Does This Sound Cuckoo to You?

A giant cuckoo clock resides within the Sierra Diablo Mountains of Texas. It is called the 10,000 year clock and it is hundreds of feet tall. "Why?" You might ask.

"I want to build a clock that ticks once a year. The century hand advances one every 100 years, the cuckoo comes out on the millennium."

The Long Now Foundation
- Creatively fostering long-term thinking

Did you know?
The largest cuckoo clock is in Amish country in Ohio.

I cannot imagine the future,
but I care about it.
Danny Hillis

No time left for you
On my way to better things
No time left for you
I found myself some wings

No time left for you
Distant roads are callin' me
No time left for you

No time for a summer friend
No time for the love you send
Seasons change and so did I
You need not wonder why.
You need not wonder why.
There's no time left for you.
No time left for you.

No time for a gentle rain
No time for my watch and chain
No time for revolving doors
No time for the killing floors.
No time for the killing floors.
There's no time left for you.
No time left for you.

No Time

-The Who

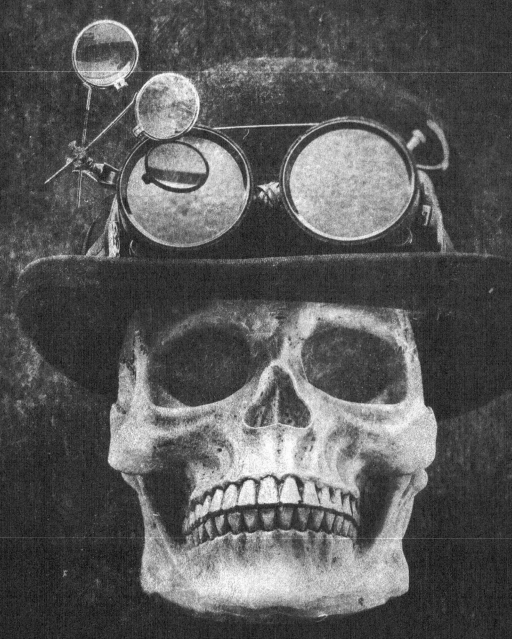

"A COMMON GENE INFLUENCES WHEN YOU WILL
WAKE UP EACH DAY AND THE TIME OF DAY YOU WILL DIE."

BONNIE PRESCOTT | NOVEMBER 26, 2012

WHEN IT'S TIME, IT'S TIME.

A Swiss study has revealed that you are 14% more likely to die on your birthday than on any other day. This study, published in the Annals of Epidemiology, analyzed 2.4 million (natural causes) deaths between 1969 and 2008. If you are over 60, the likelihood increases by 4%.

In the November 2012 issue of Annals of Neurology, a common gene variant is identified which affects circadian rhythms (or the time people die). Clifford Saper (Professor of Neurology and Neuroscience at Harvard Medical School) explains, "There is a biological clock ticking in each of us."

"The internal 'biological clock' regulates many aspects of human biology and behavior, such as preferred sleep times, times of peak cognitive performance, and the timing of many physiological processes. It also influences the timing of acute medical events like stroke and heart attack." Andrew Lim

The season of failure is the best time
for sowing the seeds of success.
Paromahonsa Yogananda

The person who has lived the most is not
the one with the most years, but the one
with the richest experiences.
Jean-Jacques Rousseau

When time is spent, Eternity begins.
Helen Hunt Jackson

Time is the wisest counselor of all.
Pericles

LEAP YEAR

Those ancient Egyptians discovered that the time required for the earth to travel around the sun is more than 365 days. In fact, it's 365 days, five hours, 48 minutes, and 46 seconds.

During the 16th century, Romans designated February 29 as leap day.

All children born on February 29 are called leaping babies and are exceptionally special. They must wait four years to celebrate their birthdays on the correct date. They do say that patience is a virtue, right?

A woman from Utah gave birth to three children, each born on February 29 – 2004, 2008, and 2012. I guess that does help with cutting back on party expenses.

LEAP TRADITIONS

Sadie Hawkins Day is synonymous with February 29. Lil' Abner must have been influenced by the Scottish Queen Margaret who declared February 29 as the day that a young women could ask a man to marry her. This commenced in 1288.

Perhaps leap year actually became "no man's land" as far back as in 5th Century Ireland. St. Patrick is said to have softened and allowed women the right to ask for a man's hand in marriage. Since priests weren't proposing, somebody had to do it.

CELEBRITIES BORN ON LEAP YEAR

1692
John Byron, English poet

1736
Ann Lee, known as the leader
of the Shakers. Her convictions
about celibacy fated the Shakers to
eventual extinction and restricted
any future " Leaping Shaker Babies"
to be born.

1904
Jimmy Dorsey, American jazz artist

1916
Dinah Shore, Actress and singer

1976
Terrence Long, Major League
baseball player

LEAP YEAR BIRTHDAYS

Most everyone shares his/her birthday with 19 million people. Leaping
babies are joined by a mere 4 million, out of a world population of 7 billion.

REALLY COOL LEAP YEAR TRIVIA

The Chinese calendar has a leap
month about every three years,
and it is named the same as the
previous lunar month. De ja vu?

The lunisolar Jewish calendar,
Adar Aleph, has a leap year seven
times in a 19-year cycle.

Time is the brush of God as
He paints his masterpiece on the
hearts of humanity.

Ravi Zacharias

Return On Investment (ROI)

By viewing time as a commodity and actions as investments, we can become more productive, thoughtful people.

Establish Multiple Positives (EMP)

Engage in an activity that generates positive return in more than one area. (Example: schedule daily exercise with friends and neighbors.)

Time is the most valuable thing a man can spend.
- *Theophrastus*

Do not squander time for that is the stuff life is made of.
- *Benjamin Franklin*

The strength of a man's virtue should not be measured by his special exertions, but by his habitual acts.
- *Blaise Pascal*

Worry does not empty tomorrow of its sorrow. It empties today of its strength.
- *Corrie Ten Boom*

The average Briton spends almost a year of their life watching soap operas according to a Dalepak research survey.

Sand & Soap

American radio programs of the 1930s became television stories in the 1950s, but some things stayed the same.

Radio and TV programs targeted women, and women love them. Soap manufacturers sponsored them and they became addictive. Soap operas, as they are now called, remain a unique phenomenon.

In the 1970s 20 million viewers were comprised of primarily women age 18 and over. By 1981, teens and men join the ranks. Evening "Soaps" like "Dallas" and "Dynasty" drew even more diversified viewers.

So what's the attraction?

Some suggestions have been offered:
- escapism • relaxation • habit
- social curiosity • a sense of extended family

"It's just a comfortable means of filling time." ...One might ask if it is filling or emptying.

"Like sands through the hourglass so are the days of our lives."
-Days of Our Lives, Long-Running Soap

"Clock" literally means "bell." Time was originally told by sounding bells, so 4 o'clock is an abbreviation of " four rings of the bell."

Clock derives from the Middle English word clokke, the old North French word cloque, and Middle Dutch's clocke.

CLOCK IDIOMS

Against the clock: Rushed and pressed for time
Race the clock: Attempt to beat a particular time
Around-the-clock: Open or continuing 24 hours a day
Like clockwork: Happening at very regular time intervals
Clock in, clock out: Record one's comings and goings
Turn back the clock: Attempts to return to the past
Beat the clock: Do something before a deadline
Clean your clock: Strike a blow to the face
A face that could stop a clock: Hideous

Time keeps on
...slippin',
...slippin',
...slippin',
into the future.

Fly Like an Eagle
The Steve Miller Band

CLOCK TRIVIA

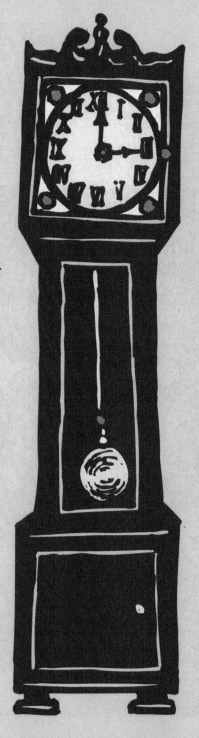

How tall is a grandfather clock?
Over 6 feet!

How tall is a grandmother clock?
It's 6 feet or under, and while
we're at it, a granddaughter clock
is less than 5 feet tall.

Is that nursery rhyme real?
There really is a hickory dickory
dock clock where a mouse
indicates the time.

What's a "wag—on—the—wall"?
A clock where the weight and
pendulum dangles uncased on
a wall.

Who made the first clock?
The first clockmaker of record in
America was Thomas Nash. New
Haven, 1638.

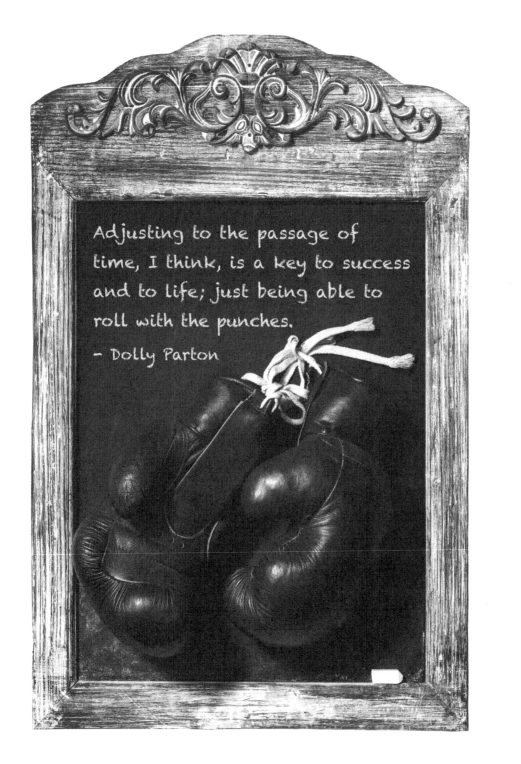

Adjusting to the passage of time, I think, is a key to success and to life; just being able to roll with the punches.

- Dolly Parton

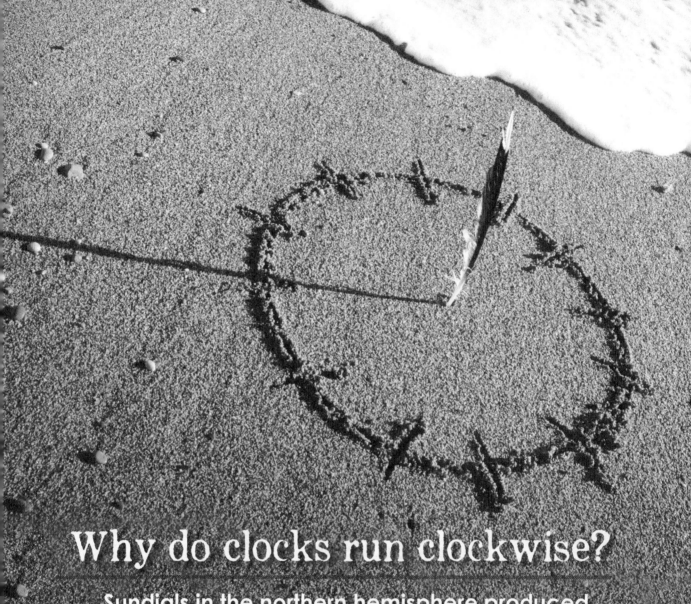

Why do clocks run clockwise?

Sundials in the northern hemisphere produced shadows that rotated "clockwise." Clock hands were built to mimic the natural movement of the sun.

HOW EASTERN CULTURES UNDERSTAND TIME

TIME IS SEEN AS CYCLICAL AND QUANTIC CONSISTING OF REPEATING AGES THAT HAPPEN TO EVERY BEING IN THE UNIVERSE BETWEEN BIRTH AND EXTINCTION.

If you are depressed,
you are living in the past.
If you are anxious,
you are living in the future.
If you are at peace,
you are living in the present.

Lao Tzu

Middle age is the awkward period when Father Time starts catching up with Mother Nature.

Harold Coffin

Beauty is unbearable, drives us to despair, offering us for a minute the glimpse of an eternity that we should like to stretch out over the whole of time.

Albert Camus

Time in a Bottle

If I could save time in a bottle
The first thing that I'd like to do
Is to save every day
'Till eternity passes away
Just to spend it with you

If I could make days last forever
If words could make wishes come true
I'd say that every day like a treasure and then,
Again, I would spend them with you

(Refrain) But there never seems to be enough time
To do the things you want to do
Once you find them
I've looked around enough to know
That you are the one I want to go
Through time with

If I had a box just for wishes
And dreams that had never come true
The box would be empty
Except for the memory
Of how they were answered by you
(Refrain)

- Jim Croce

As Time Goes By

You must remember this
A kiss is just a kiss
a sigh is just a sigh.
The fundamental things apply
As time goes by.

And when two lovers woo
They still say 'I love you'
On that you can rely.
No matter what the future brings
As time goes by.

Moonlight and love songs
Never out of date.
Hearts full of passion,
Jealousy and hate.
Woman needs man
And man must have his mate.
That no one can deny.

It's still the same old story
A fight for love and glory
A case of do or die.
The world will always welcome lovers
As time goes by.

— Herman Hupfeld

Have your moments.

Without trying we naturally spend the majority of our time consumed by our own whims and desires. Even occasional selfless giving is better than none at all. Don't be afraid to start small. Just start. There's no time like the present. Refuse to procrastinate any longer. Become a giver. Make time for someone else.

TAKE TIME

To have courage for whatever comes in life – everything lies in that.
- St. Teresa of Avila

Every time you do a good deed you shine the light a little farther into the dark. And the thing is, when you're gone that light is going to keep shining on, pushing the shadows back.
- Charles de Lint

Life is a process, and just take it a day at a time, and you can't live in tomorrow, and you can't reach back and be in yesterday. No matter how much you want to, you just have what's right here in front of you.
- Amy Grant

As you grow older you will discover that you have two hands, one for helping yourself, the other for helping others.
- Audrey Hepburn

MAKE TIME

The purpose of human life is to serve and to show compassion and the will to help others.
- Albert Schweitzer

Real generosity toward the future lies in giving all to the present.
- Albert Camus

Calendars and clocks exist to measure time, but that signifies little because we all know that an hour can seem as eternity or pass in a flash, according to how we spend it.
- Michael Ende

When I stand before God at the end of my life, I would hope that I would not have a single bit of talent left, and could say, "I used everything you gave me."
- Erma Bombeck

What do Louis XIV, the Prince of Rohan, and the King of Siam have in common?

They each owned clocks made by the elite clock company, French and Balthazar Martinot (1636-1714) The fine craftsmen, Jean-Michel Ziegler and Andre- Charles Boulle, were masters and their work can still be observed in the Louvre in Paris. (If you have time to visit)

What is Horology?

It may sound scary, but it is the art and science of making clocks.

The "Wheel of Time"

This unique and very complex teaching about the cyclical nature of time is also called Kalachokra. Similar, but often distinctively dissimilar concepts are found throughout Hinduism and various sects of Buddhism.

Time is viewed as meaningless, as is individual self-awareness. Complete separation from time is the means of spiritual purification and no "end of time" is acknowledged. Selflessness and serenity are desired.

"Time has been transformed; it has advanced and set us in motion; it has unveiled its face, inspiring us with bewilderment and exhilaration." - Khalil Gibran

It still amazes me that people spend more time researching a new vehicle than they do the religion they entrust their souls to.

Larissa Ione, Eternal Rider

Is the doctor in?
Who?
The Doctor.
Doctor Who?

"The Doctor" is the Time Lord from the planet Gallifrey.

Still behind the times? This BBC cult favorite is the most popular science-fiction television program of all times. Having first aired in 1963, it remains immensely popular.

The Doctor, a time-traveling humanoid alien, has traveled through Time Vortexes so often that he has a "special relationship" with time. In fact, such stories are too complicated for this human.

Disappointments in love, even betrayals and losses, serve the soul at the very moment they seem in life to be tragedies. The soul is partly in time and partly in eternity. We might remember the part that resides in eternity when we feel despair over the part that is in life.

Thomas Moore

The Future is, of all things, the thing least like eternity. It is the most temporal part of time – for the Past is frozen and no longer flows, and the Present is all lit up with eternal rays.

C.S. Lewis

In times of suffering illness, poverty, or misfortune, we think we shall be satisfied on the day it ceases. But thereto, we know it is false; so soon as one has gotten used to not suffering one wants something else.

Simone Weil

"Long ago, men went to sea, and women waited for them, standing on the edge of the water, scanning the horizon for the tiny ship. Now I wait for Henry. He vanishes unwillingly, without warning. I wait for him. Each moment that I wait feels like a year, an eternity. Each moment is as slow and transparent as glass. Through each moment I can see infinite moments lined up, waiting. Why has he gone where I cannot follow?"

Audrey Niffenegger, The Time Traveler's Wife

For the Present is the
point at which Time
touches Eternity.

C.S. Lewis

The training of children is a profession, where we must know how to waste time in order to save it.

Jean-Jacques Rousseau

...if anything matters then everything matters.

Because you are important, everything you do is

important. Every time you forgive, the universe changes;

every time you reach out and touch a heart or a life,

the world changes; with every kindness and service,

seen or unseen, my purposes are accomplished and

nothing will be the same again.

-Wm. Paul Young, The Shack: Where Tragedy Confronts Eternity

Even a broken clock
is right twice a day.

IS TIME OUR FRIEND OR FOE?

Ecclesiastes 3:1-11

There is an appointed time for everything
And there is a time for every event under heaven-
A time to give birth, a time to die
A time to plant, and a time to uproot what is planted,
A time to kill, and a time to heal
A time to tear down, and a time to build up
A time to weep, and a time to laugh
A time to mourn, and a time to dance
A time to throw stones, and a time to gather stones
A time to embrace, and a time to shun embracing
A time to search, and a time to give up as lost.
A time to keep, and a time to throw away
A time to tear apart, and a time to sew together
A time to be silent, and a time to speak
A time to love, and a time to hate, a time for war, and a time for peace.

What profit is there to the worker from that in which he toils? I have seen the task which God has given the sons of men with which to occupy themselves. He has made everything appropriate in its time. He has also set eternity in their heart.

He has set eternity in our heart.

Turn, turn, Turn. I grew up with this popular song by The Byrds. "There is a time for everything…." Good things happen and bad things happen, and that is (and must be) okay. Years later I discovered that the song's origin was the Bible. It comforted me as a child to believe that there was a loving and wise God in control.

Growing up in the 60s I experienced changing seasons and changing times. Sometimes I longed for change and sometimes I fought against it. Painful it often was, but I would not go back in time for anything.

The melancholy nature of Ecclesiastes can be discouraging, but I am challenged by the 11th verse.

"He has set eternity in our heart."

My heart desires a place that ceases to change. It longs for a place where relationships do not break down. I cry for an appreciation of beauty that does not become bored. Who I am and what I do MUST matter. Subtly, that "voice of eternity" in my heart promises that it does.

Eastern philosophies are rich with beauty and instruction. Serenity is attained with great sacrifice and discipline. Unfortunately, I believe that most human beings are incapable of such commitment.

But the God of Ecclesiastes can be understood by anyone, at any age, regardless of education or intellect.

I have loved many people with severe handicapping conditions. Some have mental retardation and the others, possessing very high IQs, suffer physically from cerebral palsy, spina bifida, or other challenges.

I remember the simple words of one friend. "Someday God is going to fix me," he said. "He is going to fix it all."

Time is very special for the infirmed. Especially for them, future hope gives strength to face the present.

Oh, what strange wonderful clocks women are.
They nest in Time. They make the flesh that
holds fast and binds eternity. They live inside
the gift, know power, accept, and need not
mention it. Why speak of time when you are
Time, and shape the universal moments, as they
pass, into warmth and action? How men envy
and often hate these warm clocks, these wives,
who know they will live forever.

Ray Bradbury
Something Wicked This Way Comes

"To cheat oneself out of love is the most terrible deception; it is an eternal loss for which there is no reparation, either in time or in eternity."
Søren Kierkegaard

Humans are amphibians...half spirit and half animal...as spirits they belong to the eternal world, but as animals they inhabit time. This means that while their spirit can be directed to an eternal object, their bodies, passions, and imaginations are in continual change, for to be in time, means to change.

- C.S. Lewis

If time and space, as sages say,
Are things which cannot be,
The sun which does not feel decay
No greater is than we.
So why, Love, should we ever pray
To live a century?
The butterfly that lives a day
Has lived eternally.

— T.S. Eliot

The soul exists partly in
eternity and partly in time.
- Marsilio Ficino

Love is the emblem of eternity: it confounds all notion of time: effaces all memory of a beginning, all fear of an end.

Anne-Louise-Germaine de Staël

Measured against eternity, our time on earth is
just a blink of an eye, but the consequences
of it will last forever.

Rick Warren

This day is not a sieve, losing time. With each
passing minute, each passing year, there's this
deepening awareness that I am filling, gaining time.
We stand on the brink of eternity.

Ann Voskamp

*One Thousand Gifts: A Dare to Live Fully
Right Where You Are*

"This book is for everyone who has survived. You are not broken. You can love and be loved, despite what may feel like the eternally brutal nature of the world. Even when you're drowning and so far under, there is always time to reach for someone who will teach you how to breathe again."
- Jessica Park, Left Drowning

P.S.

postscript from the author

With unending gratitude, I thank those who have taught me how to breathe again. Your love has enabled me to love, and troubled times have been softened by your touch.

To the readers who have taken the time to peruse these pages, I truly appreciate you and hope that it was time well spent – for a smile, a nod, or perhaps deep musings.

Time has altered for me on the down side of fifty. Horizons have shifted and my travel seems slowed. As a follower of the Christ of Christmas, the comfort of fullness in time seems invaluable and, therefore, worthy of sharing.

His "plan for the fullness of time, (is) to unite all things in him."(Ephesians 1:10, ESV) He is about eliminating the brutal nature of our world and filling it with love!

At this time, I offer words for consideration. I offer landscapes to fill your mind's eye. I offer hope for the weary, the drowning, the suffering.

In the words of my handicapped, but most wise friend,

The Eternal One entered time to fix us. In the fullness of time – "Someday He will fix us all!"

"Jesus' birth in Bethlehem was a moment preceded by eternity. His being neither originated in time nor came about by the will of humanity. The Author of time, who lived in the eternal, was made incarnate in time that we might live with the eternal in view. In that sense, the message of Christ was not the introduction of a religion, but an introduction to truth about reality as God alone knows it."
- Ravi Zacharias

This steampunk rabbit was designed by my sister, the lovely and talented Kathy Magee.

Steampunk and Time

The term "steampunk" appeared in the late 1980s and initially referred to a type of science fiction featuring steam-powered machinery.

Today steampunk has a loyal following in various art forms, fashion, and even as an alternative subculture.

Though trendy it seems retroactive. Victorian England meets a post-apocalyptic future. I was drawn to the old clocks, rusted gears and the surprising addition of hot air balloons and angels' wings. It seemed a fitting style for a book on time.

I have enjoyed creating many of the images featured in this book. My son Davis Skinner is credited as the esteemed photographer. I am indebted to the very talented graphic designer, Trish Diggins, and to my wonderful editor and friend, Liz Dellenbach!

KIM SKINNER

WORDS FOR WOMEN

Kim Skinner, a native Texan, started out teaching children with multiple disabilities and ended up focused on the "special needs" of women, including herself. Her inspiring message and humorous, high-energy style has delighted audiences in the U.S. and abroad. She loves cooking, quilting, and her farm animals. Her books, *A Christmas at Sea* and *Wives in the Locker Room*, are available on her website. She and her husband, David, have been married for 33 years and have five children. They live in North Florida.

kim@kimskinner.com

TWO STEPPING

MEDIA PRODUCTION

Davis Skinner is the oldest son of Kim and her husband, David. He is the CEO of Two Stepping, Inc. and an accomplished cinematographer and photographer. Using the engaging power of multimedia, Davis and his mom collaborate to share stories that will awaken, inspire and enrich. He and his wife, Janessa, reside in Jacksonville, Florida.

info@twostepping.com

CPSIA information can be obtained at www.ICGtesting.com
Printed in the USA
LVOW02*1956011214

416549LV00001B/1/P